Everybody Has Something

Story and Pictures by: **Margaret Domnick**

Margaret Domnick

First published by AuthorHouse 10/13/04

ISBN: 1-4208-0050-7 (sc)

Library of Congress Control Number: 2004097104

Printed in the United States of America
Bloomington, Indiana

This book is printed on acid-free paper.

authorHOUSE

1663 LIBERTY DRIVE
BLOOMINGTON, INDIANA 47403
(800) 839-8640
www.authorhouse.com

This book is for every child who has ever felt "different". -MD

Hi, I'm Jack.
And guess what? I have something.

My mom says that everybody has something.

Collyn

Sometimes you can see it.

Amanda

Sometimes you can't.

My sister, Jessica, is the only one in her
fourth grade class who has pimples.

And my other sister, Madeline, has bad tummy aches.

My brother, Max, has itchy skin.

Alejandra

Ali has glasses.

Adam has asthma.

I think my mom was right!
Everybody **does** have **something**.
So, what do you have?

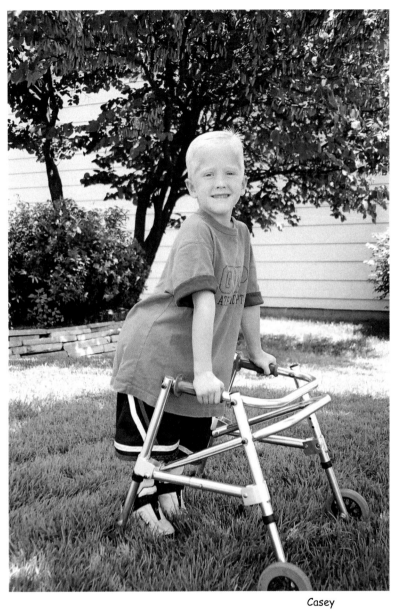

Casey

Maybe you have a walker.

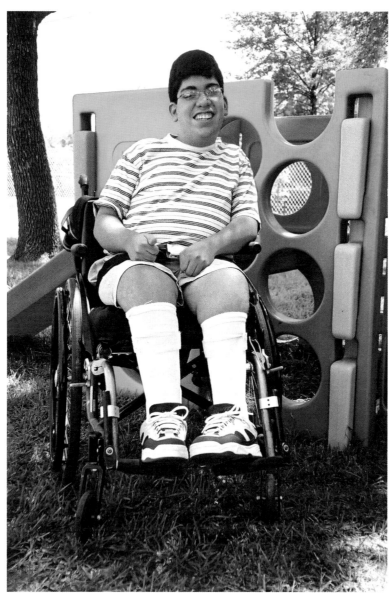

Dominic

Maybe you have a wheelchair.

Mark

Maybe you have braces on your teeth.

Jordan

Or braces on your legs.

Lexi

Maybe you have to take shots.

Riley and Rachel

Maybe you have to take blood.

Kevin

Maybe you have trouble reading.

Lindsay

Maybe you have trouble concentrating.

Adreion

Maybe you have headaches.

Ryan

Maybe you have hearing aides.

McKensie

Maybe you have allergies.

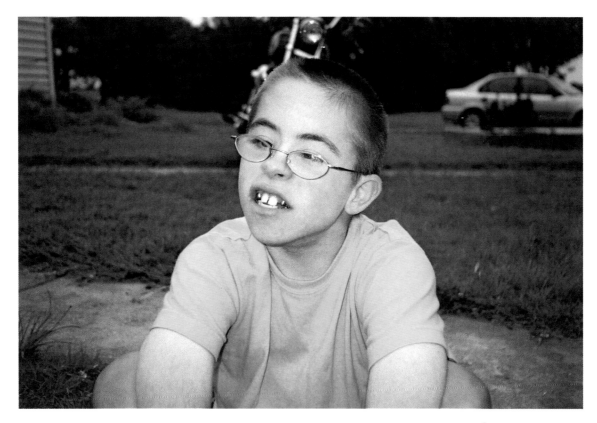

Sam

Maybe you have cavities.

Miguel

Maybe you have a cast.

Madeline

Maybe you have cancer.

Tanner and Jack

Maybe you're really tall, or really short.

Josie

Maybe you're really shy.

Domnick

Maybe you have trouble talking.

Aaron

Or maybe you have something else.

Jack

I have PKU. I have to eat a special diet.
Maybe you do too!

John

Sometimes you just don't know what a person has.
But, remember...

Everybody Has Something!

Attach photo here

Hi, my name is _____.
I have_____.
                    Maybe you do too!

Attach photo here

Hi, my name is _____.
I have_____.
Maybe you do too!

Attach photo here

Hi, my name is _____.
I have_____.
Maybe you do too!

ABOUT PHENYLKETONURIA, PKU

Phenylketonuria, commonly referred to as PKU, is a rare metabolic disorder of the liver. A person having PKU is unable to effectively use the essential amino acid phenylalanine, causing it to build-up in the bloodstream and become toxic. Since Phenylalanine is found in most foods, and must be monitored closely, it is imperative that a severely restricted diet be followed and maintained throughout a PKU person's life. PKU is genetic. It is diagnosed through newborn screening programs. If a positive screening is obtained at birth and the diet is started in the first weeks of life, and maintained appropriately, affected persons will live a healthy, normal lifestyle.

Jack Domnick has PKU. His good health is a direct result of the superior medical care offered him by the entire dedicated staff at the Inherited Metabolic Disease Clinic at Children's Hospital, Denver, CO, and from his physician at Mid-Kansas Pediatrics, Wichita, KS.

"Thank you for loving me and helping me learn about PKU. You're the BEST!" Jack

About The Author

Margaret Domnick was born and raised in Overland Park, KS. She attended Kansas State University and Wichita State University where she earned her Master of Arts degree in Speech Language Pathology.

Margaret began her book-writing career shortly after watching each of her four children struggle with issues that made them feel different. She saw a need to educate all children about diversity and acceptance, and is working toward filling that need.

Margaret has written several articles for The Harper Advocate, her local newspaper, and has coauthored a paper published in Career Development Quarterly. Margaret currently resides and writes in Harper, KS where she continues to work as a speech language pathologist in the public schools.